With **HIS** Stripes
We Are **HEALED**

With HIS Stripes
We Are HEALED

Larry Holt

Copyright © 2016 by Larry Holt.

| ISBN: | Softcover | 978-1-4931-9522-0 |
| | eBook | 978-1-4931-9521-3 |

All Bible verses taken from: King James, The Word, New International Version

Print information available on the last page.

Rev. date: 02/29/2016

To order additional copies of this book, contact:
Xlibris
1-888-795-4274
www.Xlibris.com
Orders@Xlibris.com
612104

This book is dedicated to those who are overcoming in their body with health issues spiritually, physically, and emotionally. In Revelation 12:11a it reads; "And they overcame him by the blood of the lamb and by the word of their testimony." Your confession of the word of God will bring health, healing, and wholeness.

God gave us physicians. Jesus had a physician with him his name was Luke. When you go into a doctor's office, you will see on the wall licenses to practice medicine. Doctors treat the symptoms. Jesus heals the root of the problem. The word will heal any problem that you may have. Jesus not only healed physically; He also healed the soul and spirit of a person.

I have known people who went to the doctor, and the doctor could not find anything physically wrong with them. The next step would be for them to look at the spiritual side of their life. A lot of physical and mental sickness is due to our diet. Our air is polluted, the soil is depleted from it minerals. The crops are sprayed with pesticides our water is polluted, and the chemical that is used to treat our water is not healthy. There are products in our food that is not healthy such as gluten and sugar. Our grains such as corn soybeans are Genetically Modified Organism (GMO).

Everything was given to us by God to eat according to Genesis 1:28-29, we need to go back to the beginning as originated.

May you continue to walk in the blessing of the Lord. Stay on your medication until the doctor take you off them. Remember Jesus is the Great Physician.

Introduction

The purpose of this book is to help you take God's Word around with you, and confess it at least three times a day. These confessions are based upon scriptures from the Bible.

Most christians believe that if God heals them it will be an instant healing. That is not necessarily true, because some healings are gradual. Some healings are instant, some could take one hour, one day, some one week or more. It is your faith that makes you whole.

Once you have received your healing you are accountable to maintain your healing. You have to get into a bible believing, faith teaching church. Next, you must attend classes that the church offers, and most of all you must believe and confess the word of God using the name of Jesus.

We have to confess God's Word with our mouth and believe in our hearts that the Word of God is true.

You must be persistent and bold with your confession. The word of God will always manifest itself in your body. Proverbs 4:20-22 says that, "My son attend to my saying, 21. Let them not depart from thine eyes, keep them in the midst of thine heart 22. For they are life unto those that find them and health to all of their flesh."

Nearly 2,000 plus years ago when they laid those 39 stripes on the back of Jesus, you and I were healed. All of mankind's sickness, and diseases were laid on Jesus. Because Jesus bore our sickness we no longer, have to be sick.

Due to the fall of man (Adam) sickness and disease entered into the world. It was not God's will for man to be sick. You will see in the book of Numbers chapter 21:8 "And the Lord said unto Moses, make thee a fiery serpent, and set it upon a pole; and it shall come to pass, that everyone that is bitten, when he looketh upon it shall live."

Numbers 21:9 "And Moses made a serpent of brass, and put it on a pole and it came to pass, that if a serpent had bitten any man when he beheld the serpent of brass he lived" The serpent was lifted up on a pole; Christ was lifted up on the cross.

The sick of Israel received healing by looking on the brazen serpent. People today can receive their healing by looking to Jesus Christ. The serpent itself was a symbol of sin. Christ was made sin for us that we might be made free from sin.

It has always been in the mind of God almighty that we be healed. Even in the Old Testament, he made a way of escape from sickness, and disease. The ultimate and final redemptive work was done once and for all for us through the death, burial, and resurrection of God's son, Jesus Christ.

The symbol of the serpent on the pole is used by the medical profession today.

According to Joel chapter 2 it reads "I will pour out my spirit on all flesh". In these last days God is going to demonstrate His love and power, by healing people as he did in the book of Acts. People do not have to be ill, living without limbs and confined to wheels chairs. I believe that in these last days we are to see miracles, signs and wonders as we have never seen since the beginning of time. God has many body parts stored up in heaven. I am believing God to manifest creative miracles in my ministry. I want to see blind eyes open, limbs grow where there wasn't any, deaf ears open. People getting out of wheel chairs, throwing canes away, tumors falling off this is the power we need to see in our ministries. Every church should have deliverance and healing taking place. The church is a hospital where people can come and get healed spirit, soul, and body.

The whip used were made of braided leather, with pottery shards and sharp stones affixed to the ends, which tore open the flesh of the person with each cruel swing of the whip. When we picture this terrible, inhumane form of physical punishment we look in horror. Yet the physical pain and agony was not all Jesus suffered. He took the sinfulness of mankind sins and carried them to cross willingly. Jesus knew his destiny, and He fulfilled His purpose. Will you fulfill yours? God wants to change the way christians think. God did not call the body of Christ to operate in sickness, disease, spiritual bondage, and sin. He has called us to operate in joy, peace, wisdom, health, wholeness, and all the other promises that is stated in his word. Religiosity and legalism has made the word of God of none effect. People are not aware that they have a benefit package and it is the word of God. So lets get our faith out their and believe for the super natural.

Six Reasons Why People Are Not Healed

1. Unbelief can be one of the major obstacles for someone not receiving their healing. In Matthew 13:58 "And He did not many mighty works there because of their unbelief (their lack of faith in the power of Jesus Christ").

2. Lack of knowledge can keep a person from receiving from God. Hosea 4:6 says, "My people are destroyed for lack of knowledge." Your faith cannot go beyond your knowledge.

3. Wavering will keep you from receiving your healing. You cannot have faith for the mighty working power of God to work in your life if you are double minded. James 1:8 says, "A double minded man is unstable in all his ways."

4. Failure to recognize that Satan is the author of sickness, and disease can be another reason why a person does not receive their healing. John 10:10 says that "The thief cometh not, but for to steal, kill and to destroy: I am come that they might have life, and that they might have it more abundantly." Sickness and disease come to steal kill, and destroy." God does not put sickness or disease upon people.

5. Another reason why many people are not healed is they don't have the word of God settled in their hearts. You have to find the words of God pertaining to healing and stand on those words. "Faith comes by hearing and hearing by the word of God" (Romans 10:17).

6. Another reason why people are not healed is they cannot see themselves made whole through the eyes of faith. 2 Corinthians 5:7 says," for we walk by faith, not by sight. Sickness and disease has no right to be in your body, so confess wholeness.

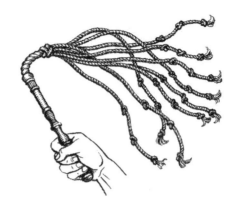

Stripe 1

According to I Peter 2:24, "Who His own self bare our sins in His own body on the tree, That we being dead to sins should live unto righteousness; by whose stripes ye were healed." Jesus bore our sickness so we no longer have to be sick.

Make this confession: I refuse all sickness, and all disease because by Jesus's stripes I am healed spirit, soul and body.

Jesus took our infirmities, and our sickness. Therefore, you and I, are completely healed from the crown of our head, to the soles of our feet.

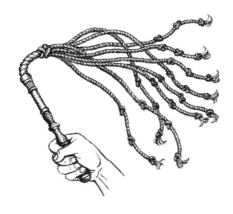

Stripe 2

According to Matthew 8:17, "That it might be fulfilled which was spoken by Esaias the prophet, saying. Himself took our infirmities and bare our sickness."

Make this confession: Body you come in the line with the word of God in the name of Jesus. I command you to function correctly in the name of Jesus.

Now command whatever weakness, sickness, or disease that you have to leave your body in the name of Jesus.

Stripe 3

According to III John 2, "Beloved, I wish above all things that thou mayest prosper and be in health even as thy soul prospereth."

Make this confession: My Jesus has healed me. Therefore, by Jesus' stripes I am healed. Yes healed from the inside out spirit, soul, and body. Thank you Jesus for healing me.

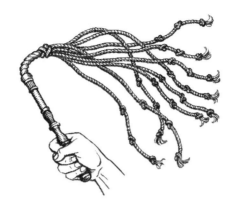

Stripe 4

According to Isaiah 53: 4-5, "Surely He hath borne our griefs and carried our sorrows; yet we did esteem him stricken smitten of God and afflicted. 5 "But he was wounded for our transgressions, he was bruised for our iniquities: the chastisement of our peace was upon him and by his stripes we are healed."

Make this confession: I can look at any sickness and disease through the eyes of faith, confess, and believe that I have received my healing in the name of Jesus. I believe I am healed based on the words of God in Jesus name.

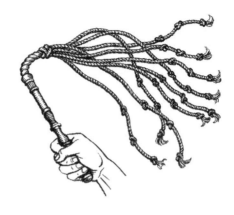

Stripe 5

According to Mark 11:22-24, "And Jesus answering saith unto them Have faith in God. 23. For verily, I say unto you, That whosoever shall say unto this mountain, Be thou removed, and be thou cast into the sea; and shall not doubt in his heart, but shall believe that those things which he saith shall come to pass; he shall have whatsoever he saith. 24. "Therefore I say unto you, What things so ever ye desire, when ye pray, believe that ye receive them, and ye shall have them."

Make this confession: Lord you said Have faith in God, Jesus I do have that faith. Jesus I speak to this mountain of (cancer, high blood, sugar diabetes, oppression, depression, low self esteem, rape, molestation, loneliness, divorce etc). Father God I thank you that these things are removed out of my life, I believe, and receive your word, and I declare that, I am healed in Jesus name, spirit soul and body. In addition, according to Psalm 107:20, "He sent his word, healed them, and delivered them from their destructions." Thank you Jesus for delivering me from destruction."

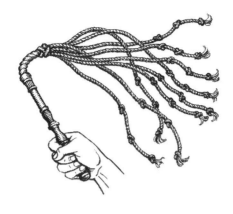

Stripe 6

According to 1 John 5:4, "For whatsoever is born of God overcometh the world: and this is the victory that overcometh the world even our faith."

Make this confession: I have overcome the world and the devil by my faith. By faith I have my healing and deliverance right now in Jesus name, body you no longer have _____ (state what problem you were having). Mind you are no longer oppressed, depressed, and filled with fear according to the Word of God because; by Jesus stripes, you are healed.

Stripe 7

According to Hebrews 11:1, "Now faith is the substance of things hoped for, the evidence of things not seen." Romans 10:17, "So then faith cometh by hearing, and hearing by the word of God."

Make this confession: Faith (God's Word) is the evidence that I have received my answer. I believe that I have received my answer by faith in Gods word. As long as I am exercising my faith, and praising God. Thank you Jesus, for healing me.

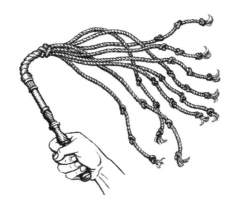

Stripe 8

According to Deuteronomy 30:19, "I call heaven and earth to record this day against you, that I have set before you life and death blessing and cursing: therefore choose life, that both thou and thy seed may live."

Psalm 103:5 "Who satifieth thy mouth with good things; so that thy youth is renewed like the eagles."

Make this confession: My heavenly Father has set life and death, blessing and cursing before me, and I choose a long life. I choose blessing in every area of my life. I choose healing and health in my spirit, soul and, body. Thank you Jesus for setting me free from all, bondages, sickness, and all disease.

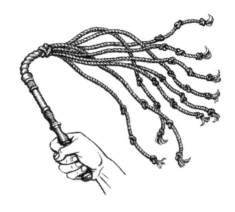

Stripe 9

According to Psalm 30:2, "O' Lord my God, I cried unto thee and thou hast healed me." Psalm 34:19, "Many are the afflictions of the righteous; but: the Lord delivereth him out of them all."

Make this confession: There is no sickness, or disease that can live in my body. Sickness and disease (name it_____). I demand you to leave my body right now in the name of Jesus. By Jesus' stripes, I am healed.

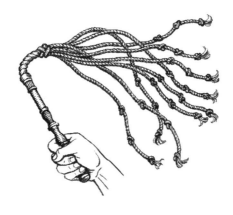

Stripe 10

According to Psalm 118:17, "I shall not die, but live, and declare the works of the Lord."

According to Proverbs 18:21, "Death and life are in the power of the tongue: they that love it shall eat the fruit there of."

Make this confession: The words of my tongue tell me I will have what I say.

Death and life are in the power of my tongue. I will make a decision to speak life to my mind and body. I speak to that mountain of sickness. Go in the name of Jesus.

Stripe 11

According to Isaiah 55:11, "So shall my word be that goeth forth out of my mouth: it shall not return unto me void, but it shall accomplish that which I please, and it shall prosper in the thing whereto I sent it."

Rev 12:11, "And they overcame him (Satan), by the blood of the Lamb and by the word of their testimony . . ."

Make this confession: I have overcome sickness and disease by the blood of Jesus Christ, and by the word of my testimony. Satan, you take your sickness and disease and leave right now in the name of Jesus Christ. Lord I return your word to you and by Jesus stripes I am healed. Philippians 4:19, "But my God shall supply all your need according to his riches in glory by Christ Jesus."

Now to seal that confession begin to praise and worship your heavenly father in the name of Jesus for meeting your need.

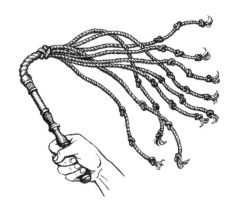

Stripe 12

According to Hebrews 4:14, "Seeing that we have a great high priest that is passed into the heavens, Jesus the Son of God let us hold fast our profession (confession)." Hebrews 10:23, "Let us hold fast the profession of our faith with out wavering (for he is faithful that promised)." Romans 4:17, Faith calls those things, which be not as though they were.

Make this confession: Lord I will hold fast to my confession of faith until my healing and deliverance is completed. I will not waiver, because every cell, organ, nerve, tissue, fiber, blood cell and all my body systems functions in the perfection which it was created to function in the name of Jesus. Body I am speaking to you, by the power of the Holy Spirit in the name of Jesus you are healed, spirit soul, and body.

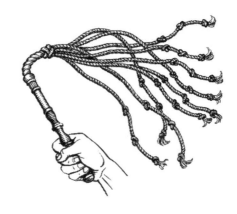

Stripe 13

According to John 10:10, "The thief cometh not, but for to, steal, and to kill, and to destroy: I am come that they might have life, and that they might have it more abundantly."

Make this confession: Jesus bring health and healing to each of us. I rebuke sickness, weakness, and disease from my body in the name of Jesus. By Jesus stripes, I am healed. I release thee, the power of God, to flow in my body everything complete and whole in Jesus name.

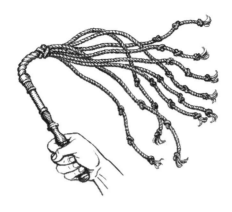

Stripe 14

"According to Isaiah 41:10, "Fear thou not for I am with thee: be not dismayed; for I am thy God: I will strengthen thee; yea, I will help thee; yea I will uphold thee with thy right hand of my righteousness."

James 4:7 "Submit yourself therefore to God. Resist the devil, and he will flee from you."

II Timothy 1:7 "For God hath not given us the spirit of fear, but of power, and of love, and of a sound mind."

Make this confession: I present my body to my Heavenly Father in the name of Jesus. I take authority, I command you spirit of fear, torment, oppression, and depression in the name of Jesus to be gone, leave me now in the name of Jesus, I speak peace, and joy in my life. I have a sound discipline mind, and I have the mind of Christ.

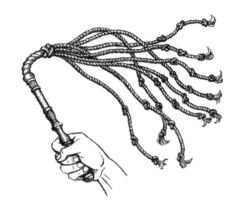

Stripe 15

According to Psalm 42:11, "Why art thou cast down, O my soul? and why art thou disquieted within me? hope thou in God: for I shall yet praise him, who is the health of my countenance, and my God."

Make this confession: Lord I thank you that my soul is not cast down. My hope is you Lord. For I will yet praise you, because you are the health of my countenance. I have peace, I refuse to worry, or be upset about anything. I am care free, worry free, burden, free, and anxiety free in Jesus name

Thank you Jesus for your peace, love, and joy that I have on the inside of me.

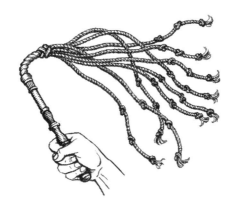

Stripe 16

According to Psalm 91:1-16, "He that dwelleth in the secret place of the most High shall abide under the shadow of the Almighty. 2. I will say of the Lord, He is my refuge and my fortress: my God; in him will I trust. 3. Surely he shall deliver thee from the snare of the fowler, and from the noisome pestilence. 4. "He shall cover thee with his feathers, and under his wings shalt thou trust; his truth shall be thy shield and buckler. 5. Thou shalt not be afraid for the terror by night; nor for the arrow that flieth by day. 6. Nor for the pestilence that walketh in darkness; nor for the destruction that wasteth at noonday. 7. A thousand shall fall at thy side, and ten thousand at thy right hand; but it shall not come nigh thee. 8. Only with thine eyes shalt thou behold and see the reward of the wicked. 9. Because thou hast made the Lord which is my refuge, even the most High, thy habitation; 10. There shall no evil befall thee, neither, shall any plague come nigh thy dwelling. 11. For he shall give his angels charge over thee, to keep thee in all thy ways. 12. They shall bear thee up in their hands, least thou dash thy foot against a stone. 13. Thou shall tread upon the lion and the addler; the young lion and the dragon shalt thou trample under feet. 14. Because he has set his love upon me, therefore will I deliver him: I will set him on high, because He has known my name. 15. He shall call upon me, and I will answer him; I will be with him in trouble; I will deliver him: and honor him. 16. With long life I will satisfy him, and shew him my salvation."

Make this confession: In the name of Jesus Christ, I take my God given authority over sickness, and disease in the name of Jesus. Sickness and disease you have no legal right to stay in my body so in the name of Jesus I demand you to leave now. I claim all healing and deliverances in the name of Jesus. There is long life in my body, not sickness and disease. Thank you Jesus for healing me.

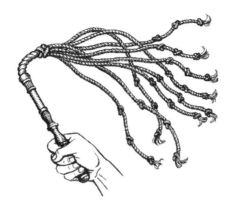

Stripe 17

According to Proverbs 17:22, "A merry heart doeth good like a medicine, but a broken spirit drieth the bones." Did you know when we laugh, exercise, and when we praise God we release a substance in our body called endorphins. This endorphin relives pain and healing and acts as medicine to the tissues of our body.

Make this confession: Heavenly Father, I praise you I thank you for delivering me and healing me. I am very happy that I am healed. Thank you for your joy that is in my heart. I give you praise honor and glory for my healing in the name of Jesus. Now give him a praise that will shake the house for what he has already done, not for what he is going to do; its already done all you have to do is believe it and receive it in Jesus name.

Stripe 18

According to Psalm 107:20, "He sent his word, healed them, and delivered them from destructions."

Make this confession: I am delivered from destruction and disease. No destruction shall come to my household in Jesus name.

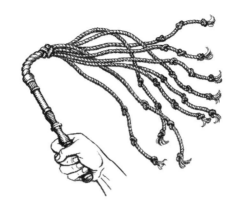

Stripe 19

According to Matthew 9:35, "And Jesus went about all the cities and villages, teaching, in their synagogues, and preaching the, gospel of the kingdom, and healing every sickness, and disease among the people." Every person who came to Jesus was completely healed. Everyone who comes to Jesus through His word for healing today is completely healed.

Make this confession: Lord Jesus I give you praise, honor, and glory for totally, and completely healing me. Every part of my body is working completely just as God had created it to do, in Jesus' name.

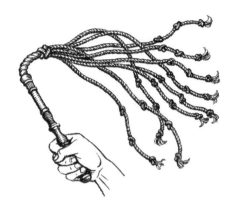

Stripe 20

According to Proverbs 3: 1-2, 8 "My son forget not my law, but let thine heart keep my commandments: 2. For length of days and long life, and peace I give unto thee. 8. It shall be health to thy navel, and marrow to thy bones."

Make this confession: As I read and meditate on your word Lord, the peace of God resides on the inside of me. While I am reading these scriptures, the peace of God is manifesting itself inside of me. Thank you Lord Jesus for your peace and joy. I have it now in the name of Jesus. There are many other scriptures that talk about peace, here are a few. John 14:27, John 16:33, and Romans 14:17.

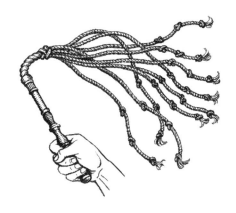

Stripe 21

According to Proverbs 4:20-22, 20 "My son attend to my words; incline thine ear unto my saying. 21. Let them not depart from the eyes; keep them in the midst of thine heart 22. For they are life unto those that find them and health to all their flesh."

Make this confession: As I keep God's word in my heart, healing is being performed. The word and my faith are working hand in hand. The word gives me long life, and health. The word of God is the solution to every problem that I might have. I am grateful that I am healed by the Blood of Jesus Christ. Thank you Jesus for setting me free and healing me, spirit, soul, and body.

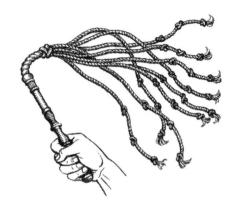

Stripe 22

According to 1 Peter 5:7, "Casting all your care upon him; for He careth for you."

Make this confession: I refuse to be upset, worried, anxious, fearful, or uptight about anything. I will only think on those things which are true, honest, just, lovely, and of a good report as in Philippians 4:8. I will only think on positive things in the name of Jesus. My mind is peaceful, quiet, and strong because I have the mind of Christ. Thank you Jesus for healing my mind, will, and emotions.

Also make this confessing: According to II Corinthians 10:5, "Casting down imaginations (reasoning's), and every high thing (thoughts, wonderings), that exalted itself against the knowledge (word) of God, and bringing into captivity every thought to the obedience of Christ."

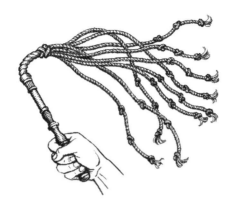

Stripe 23

According to Jeremiah 30:17, "For I will restore health unto thee, and I will heal thee of thy wounds, said the Lord."

Make this confession: Lord Jesus thank you for restoring my health and strength. Thank you for making me whole. Thank you for healing me. By Jesus stripes I am healed.

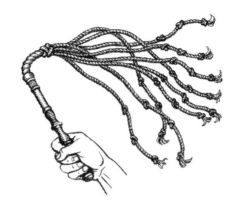

Stripe 24

According to Romans 6:14, "For sin (sickness and disease) shall not have dominion over you: for ye are not under the law, but under grace."

Make this confession: Grace is God's ability in me to do the things which I do not have the ability to do. Father God, I thank you for giving me grace. I have already received my healing.

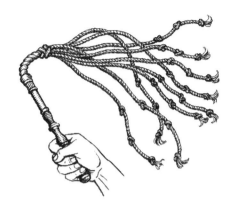

Stripe 25

According to Matthew 8:3, "And Jesus put forth his hand and touched him, saying, I will; be Thou clean. And immediately his leprosy was cleansed."

Make this confession: By Jesus stripes my body, mind, tissue, cell fiber, artery, vein, and organs is healed in the name of Jesus Christ.

Stripe 26

According to Matthew 12:15, "But when Jesus knew it, he withdrew himself from thence, and great multitudes followed him, and he healed them all." In addition, you will see in Matthew 14:14, "And Jesus went forth, and saw a great multitude, and was moved with compassion toward them, and He healed their sick."

Make this confession: Sickness I refuse to allow you to operate in my body. Jesus healed me over 2000 years ago and I rebuke every lying symptom from my body in the name of Jesus. Body you are healed in Jesus name.

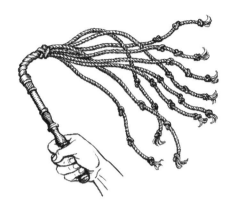

Stripe 27

According to Matthew 14:36, "And besought him that they might only touch the hem of his garment: and as many as touched were made perfectly whole."

Make this confession: I forbid any tumors, or growth, or any blood disorders of any kind to exist in my body. They dissolve, shrink, disappear and are cleansed. I am free from such activities. These disorders have no right to exist.

According to Matthew 15:13, "But he answered, and said Every plant, which my heavenly Father hath not planted, shall be up rooted." So anything that has attached itself to your body has to be rooted up in Jesus name. Father God, I thank you that my body is chemically balanced in the name of Jesus. Thank you Jesus for healing me.

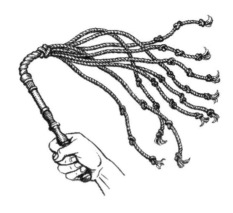

Stripe 28

According to Matthew 15:30-31, "And a great multitudes came unto him, having with them those that were lame, blind, dumb, maimed, and many others cast them down at Jesus feet; and He healed them: 31. Insomuch the multitudes wondered, when they saw the dumb to speak, the maimed to be whole, the lame to walk, and the blind to see: and they glorified the God of Israel."

Make this confession: Jesus healed the lame, blind dumb, maimed and all others who were sick. By Jesus stripes, my mind, and, body are whole and complete. I have new parts in my body. I have been restored and made new by the stripes of Jesus. Thank you Jesus for healing me.

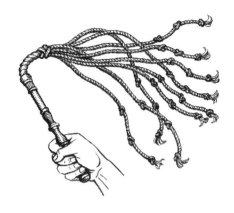

Stripe 29

According to Mark 6:56, "And whithersoever he entered, into villages, or cities, or country, they laid the sick in the streets, and besought him that they might touch if it were but the border of his garment: and as many as touched Him were made whole."

Make this confession: In the name of Jesus, I forbid any sickness, and, disease to come upon my body. Every germ, virus that touches my body dies instantly in the name of Jesus. My body is chemically balanced and, my metabolism in my body is normal in Jesus name.

Stripe 30

According to Mark 16: 17-18, "And these signs shall follow them that believe. In my name shall they cast out devils; they shall speak with new tongues; 18. They shall take up serpents; and if they drink any deadly thing it shall not hurt them; they shall lay hands on the sick and they shall recover."

Make this confession: In the name of Jesus, I lay my hands on my body and command it to be healed. As I lay my hands on my body, I command every cell, gland, organ nerve, muscle, bone ligament, joint fiber, and tissue to be made whole in the name of Jesus Christ.

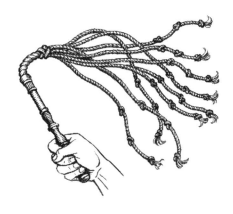

Stripe 31

According to Luke 4:40, "Now the sun was setting, all they that had sickness with divers diseases brought them unto him and he laid His hands on every one of them, and healed them."

Luke 6:10, "He said unto the man stretch forth thy hand. And he did so; and his hand was restored whole as the other."

Make this confession: Jesus your word is being formed in my body; by your stripes I am healed. My faith and your anointing shall caused growths, to disappear, tumors to shrink and die. The anointing has caused sickness, weakness and disease to flee. Thank you Jesus for setting me free.

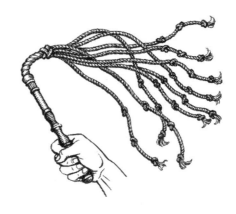

Stripe 32

According to John 14:12-13, "Verily verily, I say unto you, He that beliveth on me, the works that I do shall he do also; and greater works than these shall he do; because I go unto My Father 13. And whatsoever ye ask, command require, demand, request in My, name that will I do that the father might be glorified in the Son."

Make this confession: I believe that Jesus is my Lord and Savior, my healer, deliverer, my wisdom, and my baptizer in the Holy Spirit. I do the works of Jesus, by commanding sickness, disease, weakness, anxiety, confusion, doubt, unbelief, and worry to leave me now in the name of Jesus.

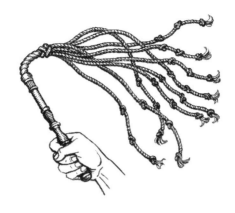

Stripe 33

According to John 15:7, "If you abide in me and my words abide in you ye shall ask what ye will, and it shall be done unto you."

Make this confession: I thank you Lord Jesus that your words abide in me; because by Jesus' stripes I am healed. I will continue to confess your words with my mouth until my healing has manifested itself. I shall continue to speak the words of God after I am healed in Jesus name.

Stripe 34

According to John 11:4, "When Jesus heard that, he said This sickness is not unto death, but for the glory of God, that the Son of God might be glorified thereby."

Make this confession: Lord Jesus I thank you that this sickness is not unto death. I thank you that you sent your word and healed me and delivered me from destruction. Lord Jesus, I thank you that I am walking in wholeness, spirit, soul and body.

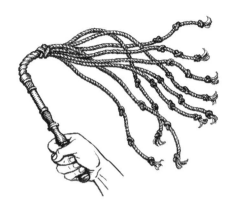

Stripe 35

According to Ephesians 4:27, "Neither give place to the devil."

Make this confession: I refuse to give place to the devil. Sickness and disease are of the devil. I refuse to give place to sickness, and disease. Satan you can't put that on my body. No sickness or plague shall come nigh my dwelling. Everything that is not of God has to leave my body in the name of Jesus.

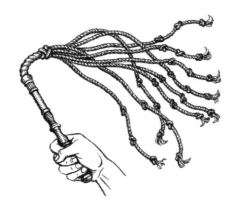

Stripe 36

According to James 4:7 "Submit yourselves therefore to God. Resist the devil, and he will flee from you."

Make this confession: I submit to the will of God. I accept the authority of God and His Word. I resist you devil; I resist all diseases in the name of Jesus.

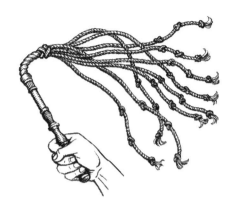

Stripe 37

According to 1 John 3:8, "He that committed sin is of the devil; for the devil sinneth from the beginning. For this purpose the Son of God was manifested, that he might destroy the works of the devil."

Make this confession: Sickness is the work of the devil. Jesus came to destroy the works of the devil. Jesus put sickness to an end for me. The activities of the devil have been undone, annulled, dissolved, and broken up in Jesus name.

Stripe 38

According to Acts 10:38, "How God anointed Jesus of Nazareth with the Holy Ghost and with power; who went about doing good and healing all that were oppressed of the devil; for God was with him."

Make this confession: Lord Jesus I thank you that I am healed from oppression, and depression. I thank you Lord for your yoke destroying, body healing anointing in Jesus name.

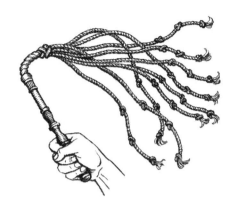

Stripe 39

According to Psalm 119:89 "For ever, O Lord thy word is settled in heaven."

Make this confession: Lord Jesus I know without a shadow of doubt that it is your will to heal. Because healing is forever settled in heaven. Jesus I thank you that you dealt with sickness and disease on the cross. I thank you, for your word is forever settled.

Now that you know God's word is settled forever, and God wants you to live free from sickness and disease. Let's take a look at how many ways to be healed.

Your Healing is God's Will

Your healing is God's will, His best for you is to have long life and finish the race. The end result is for us to be healed and others to be healed also. You have to have faith and believe that it is God's will to heal you. It is your faith that makes you whole. Your healing was completed on the cross, and you need to grab a hold of it.

Jesus purchased your healing on the cross at Calvary with his blood. When you got saved healing came along with that it was a package deal. There are many things that you can do to get healed 1. Diet and exercise, 2. Get stress and worry out of your life. 3. Get bitterness and resentment out of your life. 4. Humble yourself before God Almighty.

You can read in scripture and see that the Word of God states that healing was bought. Purchased, and paid for on the cross at Calvary. God never intended for His people to be sick with sickness and diseases. This came when Adam sinned in the garden. At that moment the devil brought in everything he could to destroy God's creation. Jesus paid the price for sin it brought Healing Peace and Deliverance.

God put together a package deal, which included forgiveness, healing, and redemption because you cannot have one without the other. God wants to restore your body to its original state that He had created it to be, nothing missing nothing broken. Healing belongs to us and is a part of our covenant with God. We are the seed of Abraham, so what God promised to Abraham we have those same promises.

The word of God tells us that if we obey His voice and follow His instructions, then He will exalt us high above everyone else. God will command His blessing on us, and our storehouses. All we need to do is accept the work that was done on the cross, which was bought and paid for by Jesus precious blood. The blessings of God are to empower, to prosper, and to supply us to have more than enough.

God does not want you sick. You have to build your inner man up daily to be able to stand up against anything that comes your way. How do you do that? By reading the word of God, confessing the word of God, and believing the word of God. If your word level is low, you cannot resist the attacks of the devil.

There has to be an understanding, and a commitment to the healing power of God in order for us to minister in His anointing effectively. Jesus was the exact representation of the will of God. You can only have faith for what you have knowledge of.

There are three areas of the Lord's body we need to understand:

1. In his body on the tree, Jesus bore our sins, and curses. If you don't understand that how can you have faith for your healing? Faith comes by hearing the Word of God. That is the only way you can mature spiritually. Faith is the only thing that is going to keep you lifted up, once again that faith is the true Word of God.

2. The main ministry Jesus did was He healed the sick, He called people to repent, He forgave people, He proclaimed His Father's Word. He bore our sickness, and carried our diseases. Through Jesus sacrifice not only provided for our redemption, He also provided eternal life. Any believer can minister the healing power of Jesus. He is no respecter of persons. God has given us the same anointing that He gave Jesus. He has commanded us to go out and preach His good news. We are to heal the sick and deliver the oppressed.

God gave us power and authority over Satan, and He has given us His anointing to heal the sick, set the captives free, and preach good news of salvation. Jesus gave us authority over all of Satan's powers and evil forces, and nothing can harm us when we are in his will. Jesus anointing, and power has been given to go, and do the work of the ministry. God is on your side all the time working on your behalf.

God backs up faith with His promises and benefits. You cannot have doubt about God and have faith. Doubt opens the door to sin, and sin opens the door for Satan to come into your life. You can find in Paul's ministry the more he did the more the devil came against him and persecuted him. Satan was the one who put the thorn in Paul's flesh. God gave him revelation on how to survive the attacks from the enemy:

1. Christ in you the hope of glory.

2. You are redeemed from the curse.

3. You have the gifts of the Spirit.

4. You are the righteousness of God

5. You are a new creation.

Through Christ, we can do all things, no matter what the devil throws our way. When the devil saw that Paul was about to break the power of darkness, he sent a messenger, or a demon to be a thorn in Paul's side. The devil gave Paul every kind of persecution, except sickness and disease. Satan could not get into Paul's body to bring physical illness.

A thorn in the flesh means something that is continually coming against you and causing you disturbance and pain.

If you are doing the work of the ministry tearing down strongholds, healing those who are sick the devil is going to bring everything he can against you. God will give you grace to press through.

The Word of God is filled with life. The Word is life and health to all your flesh when you mix it with faith. The word will produce healing, peace, and deliverance, all people have to do is reach out and take hold of it in faith just as the woman who touched the hem of Jesus' garment. God's word is a seed and it produces joy in our lives. We as believers in Jesus Christ, must understand that we are sowers who is sowing the seed of the gospel, and reaping its benefits. We need to understand that words have great power in them that will work for us or against us. I believe the majority of body of Christ their words are producing death and not life. You need to take time to examine what is coming out of your mouth is it faith or unbelief?

In our world today, man has obtained the ability to prolong life, and has healed some diseases. Jesus went through Galilee teaching, preaching the good news of the kingdom, and healing every disease and sickness. He healed every type of disease not just some of them, but all of them. The reason God wants to heal you is because He loves you and wants you to live life in health and happiness. Jesus had compassion for people and He healed them all. God's healing power is a magnet to hurting people.

Healing is not magic it comes by faith. Jesus not only healed people with His touch, but also with His words. When people were healed, it demonstrated the Kingdom of God conquering the kingdom of darkness of sickness and death. God wants you to live your life free from sickness and disease. The healing power is already operating in you all you have to do is activate it by faith. Your confession will bring your desired results.

Healing is God's divine will for you. If you have faith you have the power to do what He did. Jesus gave us several reasons why we should be healing the sick:

1. We should be doing the works that He did and even greater.

2. He gave us His anointing to heal the sick.

3. God has given a commandment to heal the sick.

4. The love of God in us should compel us to heal the sick.

The tools that we use in healing are by faith and through the Holy Spirit. We are vessels of the Lord that the Holy Spirit flows through and uses to reach hurting people in the earth.

As I have stated through the book the number one way people receive their healing by believing the promises of God in His word. You have to have faith for your miracle to manifest. God's miraculous power can work anytime, and any place. An individual's faith has to be built up and we have to bring them to what Jesus has said and what HE had done.

God's Word is true we need to pay attention to what God is saying to us through his word. The word of God has health in it and believing that it is true can heal you. The Word of God will bring life to those who find it.

Now that you know that healing is God's, will for you it is time to walk out to wholeness.

1. Recognize how you became ill.

2. Step out and deal with the issues.

3. Do not revert back to what were comfortable or old habits.

4. Give yourself time and resist temptation.

5. Remember you are the one who have to make behavior changes. How do I make behavior changes?

6. By renewing your mind by the Word of God.

I pray that this book has blessed and challenge you, and that you allow the Holy Spirit to convict and work with you, so your life can be better because God is working in your midst according to knowledge, and His good will may be performed in your live. Amen.

There are many ways to be healed here are eight ways:

1. *Serve the Lord.* Exodus 23:25 "And ye shall serve the Lord your God, and he shall bless thy bread, and thy water; and I will take sickness away from the midst of thee."

2. *Acknowledge* that healing is a benefit from God. Psalm 103:2, 3 "Praise the Lord O my soul, and forget not all his benefits, who forgives all your sins and heals all your diseases."

3. *Depart from evil.* Proverbs 3:7, 8 "Do not be wise in your own eyes; fear the Lord and shun evil. This will bring health to your body and nourishment to your bones."

4. *Meditate on the word of God.* Proverbs 4:21, 22 "Let them not depart from thine eyes; keep them in the midst of thine heart. 22. "For they are life to those who find them and health to all their flesh."

5. *Have a merry heart.* Proverbs 17:22 "A cheerful heart is medicine"

6. *Use the name of Jesus with the authority you have been given.* John 14:14 "You may ask me for anything in my name, and I will do it."

7. *Accept the anointing with oil.* Mark 6:13 "They drove out many demons and anointed many sick people with oil and healed them."

8. *Accept the laying on of hands.* Mark 12:18 "They will place their hands on sick, people and they will get well."

Sinner's Prayer

To Receive Jesus as Savior

Are you born again? Have you ever received Jesus Christ as your Lord and Savior? If the answer is no then read these scriptures.

John 3:16 "For God so loved the world, that he gave his only begotten Son, that whosoever beliveth in him should nor perish but everlasting life."

Romans 10:9-10, 13 "That if thou shalt confess with thy mouth the Lord Jesus, and shalt believe in thine heart that God hath raised him from the dead, thou shalt be saved. For with the heart man believeth unto righteousness; and with the mouth confession is made unto salvation. For whosoever shall call upon the name of the lord shall be saved."

John 14:6 "Jesus said unto him, I am the way, the truth, and the life; no man cometh unto the Father, but by me."

Now make this confession:

God, I come to you believing that Jesus Christ died on the cross for my sins. I open my heart and invite Jesus to come in to be my personal Lord and Savior. Jesus forgive me for my sins and cleanses me from all unrighteousness. Teach me your word, and fill me with the power of the Holy Spirit. Give me Godly wisdom and show me how to live a victorious life. I thank you Jesus, because I am born again and saved through your shed blood for the remission of sin. Amen

Expect A Move Of God Suddenly!

Acts 5:16 "Also a multitude gathered from the surrounding cities to Jerusalem, bringing sick people and those who were tormented by unclean spirits, and they were all healed."

Hebrews 7:25 "Wherefore he is able also to save them to the uttermost that come unto God by him, seeing he ever liveth to make intersession for them."

Acts 13:38–39 "Therefore let it be known to you, brethren, that through this Man Jesus is preached to you the forgiveness of sins; and by Him everyone who believes is justified declared righteous from all things from which you could not be justified by the law of Moses."

Romans 8:11 "But if the Spirit of Him who raised Jesus from the dead dwells in you, He who raised Christ from the dead will also give life to your mortal bodies through His Spirit who dwells in you."

2 Corinthians 4:10–11 "Always bearing about in the body the dying of the Lord Jesus that the life also of Jesus might be made manifest in our body."

Matthew 6:9–10 "Our Father in heaven, hallowed be your name. Your kingdom come. Your will be done on earth as it is in heaven."

Deuteronomy 11:21 "That your days may be multiplied, and the days of your children, in the land which the LORD sware unto your fathers to give them, as the days of heaven upon the earth."

Deuteronomy 7:15 "And the LORD will take away from you all sickness, and will afflict you with none of the terrible diseases of Egypt which you have known, but will lay them on all those who hate you."

Romans 8:32 "He that spared not his own Son, but delivered him up for us all, how shall he not with him also freely give us all things?"

Mark 16:17-18 "And these signs shall follow them that believe; In my name ... they shall lay hands on the sick, and they shall recover."

Isaiah 40:31 "But they that wait upon the Lord shall renew their strength; they shall mount up with wings as eagles; they shall run, and not be weary, and they shall walk and not faint."

Psalm 34:19 "Many are the afflictions of the righteous, but the LORD delivers him out of them all."

Jeremiah 30:17 "For I will restore health unto you, and I will heal you of your wounds, saith the Lord."

Isaiah 53:4-5 "Surely He hath borne our griefs and carried our sorrows yet we did esteem Him stricken, smitten of God and afflicted. But He was wounded for our transgressions, He was bruised for our iniquities; the chastisement of our peace was upon Him; and by His stripes we are healed."

Jeremiah 33:6 "Behold, I will bring you health and cure, and I will cure you, and will reveal unto you the abundance of peace and truth."

Matthew 18:19 "Again I say to you that if two of you agree on earth concerning anything that they ask, it will be done for them by My Father in heaven."

Mark 11:24 "Therefore I say to you whatever things you ask when you pray, believe that you receive them, and you will have them."

Isaiah 58:8 "Thy light shall break forth as the morning, and thy health shall spring forth speedily; and thy righteousness shall go before thee: the glory of the Lord shall be thy rear guard."

Psalm 41:3 (Amplified Version) "The Lord will sustain, refresh, and strengthen him on his bed of languishing; all his bed You O Lord will turn, change, and transform in his illness."

1 Thessalonians 5:23 "And the very God of peace sanctify you wholly completely; and I pray God your whole spirit and soul and body be preserved blameless sound, complete and intact unto the coming of our Lord Jesus Christ."

1 Peter 2:24 "Who Himself bore our sins in His own body on the tree, that we, having died to sins, might live for righteousness by whose stripes you were healed."

"Psalm 103:2-3 "Bless the Lord, O my soul, and forget not all His benefits: Who forgiveth all thine iniquities; who heals all thy diseases"

3 John 2 "Beloved, I wish above all things that thou mayest prosper and be in health, even as thy soul prospereth."

Jeremiah 17:14 "Heal me, O LORD, and I shall be healed; save me, and I shall be saved: for thou art my praise."

James 5:14-15 "Is any sick among you? Let him call for the elders of the church; and let them pray over him, anointing him with oil in the name of the Lord: And the prayer of faith shall save the sick, and the Lord shall raise him up; and if he have committed sins, they shall be forgiven him."

1 Thessalonians 5:8-10 "But let us who are of the day in Christ be sober Word minded, putting on the breastplate of faith and love, and as a helmet the hope of salvation 9. For God did not appoint us to wrath [the curse], but to obtain salvation through our Lord Jesus Christ."

Use Your Authority and Resist Fear!

Matthew 18:18 "Verily I say unto you, whatsoever you shall bind on earth shall be bound in heaven: and whatsoever you shall loose on earth shall be loosed in heaven."

John 10:10 "The thief Satan does not come except to steal, and to kill, and to destroy. I Jesus have come that they may have life, and that they may have it more abundantly."

Luke 10:19 "Behold, I give unto you authority to tread on serpents and scorpions, and over all the power of the enemy: and nothing shall by any means hurt you."

Isaiah 41:10 "So do not fear, for I am with you; do not be dismayed, for I am your God. I will strengthen you and help you; I will uphold you with my righteous right hand."

Isaiah 54:17 "No weapon formed against you shall prosper, and every tongue which rises against you in judgment YOU shall condemn. This is the heritage birthright of the servants of the LORD, and their righteousness is from Me," says the LORD."

You Are An Overcomer Through Jesus Christ!

1 John 4:4 ".... Greater is he that is in you, than he that is in the world."

1 John 5:4 "For whatsoever is born of God overcometh the world: and this is the victory that overcometh the world, even our faith."

Romans 8:31 "What shall we then say to these things? If God be for us, who can be against us?"

1 John 4:17 "Love has been perfected among us in this: that we may have boldness in the day of judgment; because as He is, so are we in this world."

1 Corinthians 6:15-17 "Do you not know that your bodies are members of Christ? Shall I then take the members of Christ and make them members of a harlot? Certainly not! Or do you not know that he who is joined to a harlot is one body with her? For "the two," He says, "shall become one flesh." But he who is joined to the Lord is one spirit with Him."

2 Peter 1:3-4 "As His divine power has given to us all things that pertain to life and godliness, through the knowledge of Him who called us by glory and virtue, by which have been given to us exceedingly great and precious promises, that through these you may be partakers of the divine nature, having escaped the corruption that is in the world through lust."

1 Corinthians 1:9 "God is faithful, by whom you were called into the fellowship of His Son, Jesus Christ our Lord."

Romans 5:17 "For if by the one man's offense Adam death reigned through the one, much more those who receive abundance of grace and of the gift of righteousness will reign in life through the one, Jesus Christ."

Genesis 1:28 "And God blessed them, and God said unto them, Be fruitful, and multiply, and replenish the earth, and subdue it: and have dominion over the fish of the sea, and over the fowl of the air, and over every living thing that moveth upon the earth."

Colossians 1:13 "He has delivered us from the power of darkness and conveyed us into the kingdom of the Son of His love."

Make Jesus The Lord Of Your Life; Reverence Him By Closing All Doors To The Enemy, Giving Him First Place!

Proverbs 3:7-8 "Do not be wise in your own eyes; fear the LORD and depart from evil. It will be health to your flesh, and strength to your bones."

Exodus 15:26 "If thou will diligently harken to the voice of the Lord thy God, and wilt do that which is right in His sight, and wilt give ear to His commandments, and keep all His statutes, I will permit none of these diseases upon thee, which I have brought upon the Egyptians: for I am the Lord that healeth thee."

Exodus 23:25 "So you shall serve worship the Lord your God and He will bless your bread and your water. And I will take sickness away from the midst of you."

Psalm 91:9-10 "Because thou hast made the LORD, which is my refuge, even the Most High, thy habitation; There shall no evil befall thee, neither shall any plague come nigh thy dwelling."

Malachi 4:2-3 "But unto you that fear reverence, worship My name shall the Sun of Righteousness arise with healing in His wings; and you shall go forth, and grow up as calves of the stall. You shall trample the wicked for they shall be ashes under the soles of your feet on the day that I do this says the Lord of hosts."

Know That When You Ask The Lord For Healing, It Is Already His Will And He Hears You And He Agrees. Know He Has Already Settled It In The Atonement Of The Blood Of Jesus Christ.

Psalm 30:2 "O LORD my God, I cried unto thee, and thou hast healed me."

Psalm 107:19-20 "Then they cry unto the LORD in their trouble, and he saveth them out of their distresses. He sent his word, and healed them, and delivered them from their destructions."

Matthew 7:7-8 "Ask, and it will be given to you; seek, and you will find; knock, and it will be opened to you. For everyone who asks receives, and he who seeks finds, and to him who knocks it will be opened."

I John 5:14-15 "Now this is the confidence that we have in Him, that if we ask anything according to His will, He hears us. And if we know that He hears us, whatever we ask, we know that we have the petitions that we have asked of Him."

2 Corinthians 1:20 "For all the promises of God in Him are Yes, and in Him Amen, to the glory of God through us." *Psalm 35:27* "Let them shout for joy and be glad, Who favor my righteous cause; And let them say continually, "Let the LORD be magnified, Who has pleasure in the prosperity of His servant."

The Will Of God Is His Blessing Of Goodness That Is For You Now!

Jeremiah 29:11 "For I know the thoughts that I think toward you, says the Lord, thoughts of peace and not of evil, to give you a future and a hope an expected end."

Luke 12:32 "Do not fear, little flock, for it is your Father's good pleasure to give you the kingdom."

Psalm 121:7-8 "The Lord shall preserve keep you from all evil; He shall preserve your soul life. The Lord shall preserve your going out and your coming in from this time forth and even forevermore."

Hebrews 13:20-21 (Amplified Version) "Now may the God of peace [Who is the Author and the Giver of peace], Who brought again from among the dead our Lord Jesus, that great Shepherd of the sheep, by the blood that sealed, ratified the everlasting agreement covenant, testament, strengthen complete, perfect and what you ought to be and equip you with, everything good that you may carry out His will; while He Himself works in you and accomplishes that which is pleasing in His sight, through Jesus Christ the Messiah; to Whom be the glory forever and ever to the ages of the ages."

The Word Of God Brings Healing!

Psalm 119:50 "This is my comfort in my affliction, for your Word has given my life."

Romans 10:17 "So then faith comes by hearing and hearing by the word of God."

Proverbs 4:20-22 "My Son, attend to My words; incline thine ear unto My sayings. Let them not depart from thine eyes; keep them in the midst of thine heart. For they are life unto those that find them, and health to all their flesh."

John 8:32 "And ye shall know the truth, and the truth shall make you free."

Jeremiah 23:29 "Is not My word like a fire? says the LORD, And like a hammer that breaks the rock in pieces?"

2 Timothy 3:16-17 "All Scripture is given by inspiration of God, and is profitable for doctrine, for reproof, for correction, for instruction in righteousness, that the man of God may be complete, thoroughly equipped for every good work."

John 6:63 "It is the Spirit who gives life; the flesh profits nothing. The words that I speak to you are spirit, and they are life."

John 15:7 "If you abide in Me, and My words abide in you, you will ask what you desire, and it shall be done for you."

Isaiah 55:11 "So shall my word be that goeth forth out of my mouth: it shall not return unto me void, but it shall accomplish that which I please, and it shall prosper in the thing whereto I sent it."

Jeremiah 1:12 "I am alert and active watching over My Word to perform it." Amplified Bible

Joshua 21:45 "Not a word failed of any good thing which the LORD had spoken to the house of Israel. All came to pass."

Leviticus 18:4-5 "You shall observe My judgments and keep My ordinances, to walk in them: I am the Lord of your God. 5 You shall therefore keep My statutes and My judgments, which if a man does, he shall live by them: I am the Lord!" This not only includes healing and health but all other areas of our life as well, financial, emotional, relational, intellectual, etc.

Healing Is A Good Gift From God!

James 1:17 "Every good gift and every perfect gift is from above, and cometh down from the Father of lights, with whom is no variableness, neither shadow of turning."

1 Corinthians 3:21-22 "Therefore let no one boast in men. For all things are yours: whether Paul or Apollos or Cephas, or the world or life or death, or things present or things to come—all are yours."

Romans 11:29 "For the gifts and the calling of God are irrevocable."

Philippians 2:13 "For it is God who works in you both to will and to do for his good pleasure."

Matthew 11:28 (Amplified Version) "Come to Me, all you who labor and are heavy-laden and overburdened, and I will cause you to rest. I will ease and relieve and refresh your souls."

Deuteronomy 29:29 "The secret things belong to the Lord our God, but those things which are revealed belong to us and to our children forever, that we may do all the words of this law."

Isaiah 33:24 "And the inhabitant will not say, "I am sick"; the people who dwell in it Zion will be forgiven their iniquity."

We Have Been Redeemed Out From Under The Curse Of Sickness & Disease.

Galatians 3:13-14 "Christ hath redeemed us from the curse of the law, being made a curse for us; for it is written, Cursed is every one that hangeth on a tree: That the blessings of Abraham might come on the Gentiles through Jesus Christ."

Proverbs 26:2 "Like a flitting sparrow, like a flying swallow, so a curse without cause shall not alight."

Romans 8:2 "For the law of the Spirit of life in Christ Jesus has made me free from the law of sin and death."

Colossians 1:13 "He has delivered us from the power of darkness and conveyed us into the kingdom of the Son of His love."

1 John 3:8b "For this purpose the Son of God was manifested, that He might destroy the works of the devil." Take a look at this same verse in the Amplified version "The reason the Son of God was made manifest visible was to undo, destroy, loosen, and dissolve the works the devil has done."

2 Corinthians 3:17 "Now the Lord is the Spirit; and where the Spirit of the Lord is, there is liberty."

John 8:36 "Therefore if the Son makes you free, you shall be free indeed."

Your Attitude Will Determine Your Destiny

Hebrews 12:12–13 "Wherefore lift up the hands which hang down, and the feeble knees; And make straight paths for your feet, lest that which is lame be turned out of the way; but let it rather be healed."

Psalm 42:11 "Why art thou cast down, O my soul? and why art thou disquieted within me? Hope thou in God: for I shall yet praise him, who is the health of my countenance, and my God."

We Can Have Confidence in God, For God Cannot Lie

Hebrews 10:23 "Let us hold fast the profession of our faith without wavering; for he is faithful that promised" impossible for God to lie!

I John 5:14–15 "Now this is the confidence that we have in Him, that if we ask anything according to His will, He hears us. And if we know that He hears us, whatever we ask, we know that we have the petitions that we have asked of Him."

Hebrews 10:35–36 "Therefore do not cast away your confidence, which has great reward. For you have need of endurance, so that after you have done the will of God, you may receive the promise."

Long Life Belongs to You Base Your Faith in the Word The Will Of God

Genesis 6:3   And the LORD said, "My Spirit shall not strive with man forever, for he is indeed flesh; yet his days shall be one hundred and twenty years."

Psalm 90:10   "The days of our lives are seventy years; and if by reason of strength they are eighty years, yet their boast is only labor and sorrow; for it is soon cut off, and we fly away."

Deuteronomy 30:19–20   "I call heaven and earth as witnesses today against you, that I have set before you life and death, blessing and cursing; therefore that both you and your descendants may live; that you may love the LORD your God, that you may obey His voice, and that you may cling to Him, for He is your life and the length of your days; and that you may dwell in the land which the LORD swore to your fathers, to Abraham, Isaac, and Jacob, to give them."

Psalm 91:16   "With long life I will satisfy him, and show him my salvation."

Psalm 118:17   "I shall not die, but live, and declare the works of the LORD."

Cast Down All Thoughts and Imaginations That Do not Line Up With The Word Of God

2 Corinthians 10:4–5   "For the weapons of our warfare are not carnal, but mighty through God to the pulling down of strong holds ; Casting down imaginations, and every high thing that exalted itself against the knowledge of God, and bringing into captivity every thought to the obedience of Christ."

Make your request to God

Isaiah 43:25-26 "I, even I, am He who blots out your transgressions for My own sake; and I will not remember your sins. Put Me in remembrance; let us contend together; state your case, that you may be acquitted."

Your Words Are Important

Isaiah 57:19 "I create the fruit of the lips; Peace, peace to him that is far off, and to him that is near, saith the LORD; and I will heal him."

Mark 11:22-23 "And Jesus answering saith unto them, have faith in God. For verily I say unto you, That whosoever shall say unto this mountain, Be thou removed, and be thou cast into the sea; and shall not doubt in his heart, but shall believe that those things which he saith shall come to pass; he shall have whatsoever he saith."

Job 22:26-28 "For then you will delight in the Almighty, and lift up your face to God. You will pray to Him, and He will hear you; and you will pay your vows. You will also decree a thing, and it will be established for you; and light will shine on your ways."

Remember To Give Testimony of Your Healing

Revelation 12:11 "And they overcame him by the blood of the Lamb and by the word of their testimony . . ." Hold On To Your Healing

Nahum 1:7,9b "The LORD is good, a stronghold in the day of trouble; and He knows those who trust in Him. He will make an utter end of it. Affliction will not rise up a second time."

Stay on your medication until your doctor take you off.

Testimonials

You will see in Acts 10:38 "How God anointed Jesus of Nazareth with the Holy Ghost and with power; who went about doing good, and healing all that were oppressed of the devil, for God was with him." We as believers have that same anointing, and power to do what Jesus did, Here are some accounts that happen in our ministry.

Nineteen ninety-six Madisonville, KY a couple could not conceive, I prayed for them and a year later, they had a child.

Nineteen ninety-eight Evansville, IN a Pastor friend of ours called and said that someone they knew was dying. Hospice was called in. When we arrived the woman was laying on the floor in the living room. Then we prayed the word of God over this woman. The next day she was up and doing well.

Two thousand one Henderson KY one of my wife's friend father had lung cancer. We prayed for him on a couple occasion. God healed him. The next time we went to see him he was up and traveling to another state.

Nineteen Ninety Three Madisonville, KY I received Jesus as my Savior and was immediately healed from a childhood disease I had suffered with which was asthma. Medical science has no cure for this.

Two thousand five Kingston Jamaica, my wife, and I were on a mission trip. There was a woman who was deaf in one ear. We prayed the word of God over her, and her hearing was restored immediately.

Two thousand eight Nashville, TN my Pastor and I went to the VA hospital and prayed for a man whose brain was swollen and he was in a coma. We prayed the word of God over him and within a week, and he was released from the hospital healed.

Two thousand nine Nigeria Africa, my wife and I was on a mission trip There was a Pastor in our class who had malaria. We were not teaching on healing, but the grace of God healed him.

That same day God gave me a scripture to give to his wife. She had been sick all week. The scripture is in Exodus 23:25 and it reads, "And ye shall serve the Lord your God, and he shall bless thy bread and thy water; and I will take sickness away from the midst of thee."

In a world of contaminated water and bread, praying this scripture over their bread and water God protected them and healed his wife of her disease that day.

Two thousand eleven Nashville, TN my Pastor and his wife and my wife went to a hospital to pray for a man who had a couple of aneurysm. The doctor told him if he left the hospital that he would die. The medical team could not get his blood pressure down, and he had not slept in days. As we began to lay hands on him, he went out under the power of God. Right after that, the nurse came in to take his vitals his blood pressure and it was normal. Two days later, he was out of the hospital healed.

Two thousand twelve Nashville, TN my Pastor and I went to the hospital to pray for a lady who was in a coma. Three days later, she was out of ICU and on a regular floor. A week later she was back in ICU we went back and prayed for her once again. She is out of the hospital and back to work.

Two thousand thirteen Madison, TN there was a woman that came to our church using a cane to help her walk. We prayed for her and she was healed.

Two thousand thirteen Madison, TN there is a woman in our church who had bladder cancer after prayer she was healed.

Two thousand thirteen Goodlettsville, TN I prayed for a four month old baby who had a heart murmur. The mother took the baby back to the doctor and the murmur was not there.

Two thousand fourteen Hendersonville, TN I went to my doctor for a checkup. He said that he was having problems with his right hip. I prayed for him and he received his healing. These are a few accounts of how God has healed his people.

Two thousand thirteen Madison TN, my Bishop had a colonoscopy. They found a mass in his colon. The doctor wanted him to have surgery he refused. Within two weeks Bishop passed that mass. God had healed his body.

Two thousand thirteen Madison TN, there is a lady in our church who had breast cancer was healed.

In our ministry healing takes place often because we allow the Holy Spirit to operate in our services. We tell people to stay on their medication until the doctor gives them the clearance to get off of them.

Summary

How God Viewed Sickness

Sickness destroys the body as sin destroys the spirit. Disease steals health, peace, money, health, time, and employment. God calls sickness captivity. Jesus came to preach deliverance to the captives. Jesus called sickness bondage. Jesus came to set people free with the truth. Jesus viewed sickness as oppression, and healed those who were oppressed. The bible identifies death as an enemy. Sickness is called, loathsome which means; very bad, disgusting, or repulsive. Sickness is also viewed as evil and deadly.

Their are two laws in operation in our universe spiritual and natural. Spiritual law deals with the things of the spirit which is sin.

God has natural law when this law is violated sickness in the body is the result of this violation. What are some of the natural laws? I am glad you asked;

1. Improper diet

2. Lack of exercise

3. Abuse of drugs and alcohol

4. Lack of Godly relationship with others, (doing away with bitterness and unforgiveness).

So let us get our temple in proper working order so we can do the work of the kingdom.

This book was written to give people hope through the word of God pertaining to health and healing. I myself was heal from asthma which I had from child hood. Through the word of God confessing scripture and believing what the word of God says my healing was manifested. Jesus took 39 strips on his back for our healing and by his strips we are healed. Acts 10:38 How God anointed Jesus of Nazareth with the Holy Ghost and with power, who went about doing good, and healing all that were oppressed of the devil; for God was with him. Those who read this book stay on your medication until your doctor give you the all clear. Jesus wants you to be healed spirit, soul, and body.

About the Author

Larry Holt was born and raised in Toledo, Ohio. He joined the US Army at the age of seventeen, where he spent his next twenty years. Larry retired in 1985 and enrolled at Brescia University. In 1989, he earned his bachelor of arts degree in Sociology and Psychology from Brescia University in Owensboro, Kentucky. Larry and his wife Kathy desire to see people healed just as Jesus does.

Printed in Great Britain
by Amazon